PRINCEWILL LAGANG

Love Letters to Jesus: Christian Dating Devotions

First published by PRINCEWILL LAGANG 2023

Copyright © 2023 by Princewill Lagang

All rights reserved. No part of this publication may be reproduced, stored or transmitted in any form or by any means, electronic, mechanical, photocopying, recording, scanning, or otherwise without written permission from the publisher. It is illegal to copy this book, post it to a website, or distribute it by any other means without permission.

Princewill Lagang asserts the moral right to be identified as the author of this work.

First edition

This book was professionally typeset on Reedsy.
Find out more at reedsy.com

Contents

1	The Quest for Love	1
2	Preparing the Soil	4
3	Navigating the Dating World	7
4	Building a Christ-Centered Relationship	10
5	Nurturing a Love that Reflects God's Love	14
6	Facing Challenges and Growing Together	18
7	Celebrating Milestones and Looking Ahead	22
8	A Lifetime of Love	26
9	The Power of Prayer and Perseverance	30
10	A Legacy of Love	34
11	Endless Love and Gratitude	38
12	A Journey of Worship and Ongoing Devotion	42

1

The Quest for Love

Title: "Love Letters to Jesus: Christian Dating Devotions"

In the quiet sanctuary of her favorite coffee shop, Emily sat with her journal open before her. The soft aroma of freshly brewed coffee wafted through the air, the gentle hum of conversation surrounded her, but her focus remained undivided. She dipped her pen into the inkwell of her heart and began to write, the words flowing like a river.

"Dear Jesus,

I've embarked on a journey, one that countless others before me have taken. A quest for love, not just any love, but the kind that's deep, profound, and rooted in You. I know that You are the ultimate source of love, and I want my dating life to reflect Your light and truth.

In this journey, I seek to be guided by Your wisdom, inspired by Your grace, and strengthened by Your love. For far too long, I've allowed the world to dictate what love should be, but I'm ready to surrender my heart to Your plans.

LOVE LETTERS TO JESUS: CHRISTIAN DATING DEVOTIONS

I've often heard that the first step in finding the love I desire is to fall in love with You, and I'm determined to do just that. As I pen down these words, I'm reminded of your unwavering, boundless love. The love that forgives, the love that heals, the love that redeems. It's this love I want to experience in my dating life.

In a world full of dating apps, swipes, and fleeting connections, it's easy to get lost in the search for human love. But I want my heart to be centered on You, knowing that the love story You write for me is far greater than any romance I could ever imagine. I want my dating journey to be a reflection of Your love, a testament to Your grace.

As I prepare for this journey, I also recognize my imperfections, my insecurities, and my need for Your guidance. Help me, Lord, to seek self-awareness, to grow in character, and to be the kind of partner that aligns with Your heart. Whether or not I've already met the one You've planned for me, I want to be the best version of myself for that person and for You.

I ask for Your guidance as I navigate the world of Christian dating. Give me discernment to recognize Your voice when making choices, whether it's deciding to start a new relationship, facing challenges within a current one, or even making the choice to be single if that's what You have in store for me. I trust in Your timing and Your wisdom.

Help me to surround myself with a supportive community of believers who share my values, and together, we can grow in faith and love. I know that this journey won't always be easy, but I'm determined to face the trials and tribulations with faith and grace, just as You did.

In these love letters to You, Jesus, I hope to chronicle my journey, seeking Your guidance, wisdom, and love. Through prayer, reflection, and devotion, I want to make my dating life a testament to Your glory.

Amen."

As Emily finished writing, she felt a renewed sense of purpose. She knew that her journey to find love wasn't going to be a simple one, but with Jesus by her side, she was ready to embrace it. With her love letters to Jesus in hand, she took a sip of her coffee, closed her journal, and prepared to embark on a path of Christian dating and devotion.

2

Preparing the Soil

Title: "Love Letters to Jesus: Christian Dating Devotions"

Emily had started her journey with her heart's inkwell filled with devotion and prayer. In the weeks that followed her first love letter to Jesus, she began to realize that the path to love was not just about finding someone special; it was also about preparing herself for the love God had planned for her.

With each new day, Emily felt a deepening connection to her faith, and her love letters to Jesus became a constant source of inspiration and guidance. This chapter in her journey would focus on preparing her heart and mind for the love story she hoped to share with the right person.

1. Self-Reflection: Digging Deep

One of the first steps Emily took was to dive deep into self-reflection. She knew that before she could truly love another person, she needed to love herself and understand her own heart. So she wrote to Jesus:

"Dear Jesus,

In my quest for love, I've realized that the love story I long for starts within me. To love another as You love us, I must learn to love myself in Your image. Help me, Lord, to see myself as You see me - a precious child of God, worthy of love and respect.

I'm starting this journey of self-reflection, peeling back the layers of my heart, understanding my fears, insecurities, and past wounds. I want to confront these vulnerabilities, not with shame, but with Your grace, so I can heal and grow.

Guide me as I examine my past relationships and learn from both the triumphs and the failures. Show me the patterns that need to be broken, and reveal the strengths that I can build upon. With Your help, I can leave behind any baggage that may hinder me from embracing the love You have in store.

Amen."

2. Faith in God's Timing: Patience in the Waiting

As Emily delved into self-reflection, she also needed to grapple with patience, knowing that God's timing was perfect. She wrote:

"Dear Jesus,

In a world of instant gratification, it's not always easy to wait for Your perfect timing. But I trust in Your divine plan, and I know that waiting is not wasting. It's a time for growth, learning, and becoming the person You want me to be.

Help me to find contentment in this season of waiting, not as a passive onlooker but as an active participant in Your divine plan. Grant me the patience to wait for the person who aligns with Your purpose for my life. I'm ready to let go of any desperate striving and to embrace Your timing.

Keep my heart open and my faith strong. Remind me that, just as You are preparing me, You are also preparing the one meant for me.

Amen."

3. Embracing Community: A Supportive Network

Emily knew she couldn't walk this path alone. She sought the support of a close-knit Christian community. She penned a letter to Jesus:

"Dear Jesus,

I'm grateful for the community of believers You've placed in my life. They encourage me, challenge me, and pray for me. In my pursuit of love, I want to continue to cultivate these relationships and let them shape my journey.

Guide me in finding mentors, friends, and accountability partners who can walk with me on this path. Help me create a strong support system that will provide me with wisdom, encouragement, and guidance.

May our fellowship be centered on You, Jesus, and Your love, and may it strengthen me for the journey ahead.

Amen."

As Emily concluded her second love letter to Jesus, she felt a sense of empowerment. Preparing the soil of her heart was an ongoing process, but it was one filled with faith, hope, and a deepening connection to God. She knew that the journey ahead might be challenging, but she was ready to embrace it with open arms, knowing that she was on the path to discovering the love God had planned for her.

3

Navigating the Dating World

Title: "Love Letters to Jesus: Christian Dating Devotions"

As Emily continued her journey in search of love rooted in faith, her focus shifted toward the practical aspects of Christian dating. In this chapter, she explored how to navigate the complexities of the dating world while staying true to her values and devotion to Jesus.

1. Defining Your Values and Boundaries

Before she could even think about dating, Emily realized the importance of defining her values and boundaries. In her love letter to Jesus, she wrote:

"Dear Jesus,

In the world of dating, it's easy to be swayed by the values and expectations of others. I want to establish my own set of values, firmly rooted in You. Help me define what is non-negotiable and what I can be flexible on.

Guide me in setting clear boundaries that protect my heart and honor You.

Give me the strength to communicate these boundaries respectfully and assertively with potential partners.

I want my dating journey to be a reflection of my faith, and I need Your guidance in setting those boundaries.

Amen."

2. Seeking Compatibility and Shared Faith

Emily knew the importance of finding someone who shared her faith. In her letter to Jesus, she expressed her hopes:

"Dear Jesus,

I believe that a shared faith is the foundation of a strong and lasting relationship. Help me to seek compatibility beyond surface qualities. Let me find someone who is not only attractive but also shares my love for You.

Guide me to be discerning in my choices, to see beyond the surface, and to look for signs of a genuine, Christ-centered faith in a potential partner. Lead me toward someone who can support my spiritual growth and encourage me in my devotion to You.

Amen."

3. Patience and Trust in God's Plan

Navigating the dating world could be frustrating, but Emily's faith reminded her to be patient and trust in God's plan:

"Dear Jesus,

Sometimes, it's difficult to stay patient in the quest for love. The pressures of the world and the desire for companionship can be overwhelming. But I know that Your timing is perfect, and I trust in Your plan.

Help me to remember that each step on this journey is part of Your divine design. Whether I'm in a season of waiting or actively dating, remind me that You are in control, and Your plan is unfolding.

I place my trust in You, Jesus, and I'm ready to embrace each twist and turn in the path You have laid out for me.

Amen."

As Emily completed her third love letter to Jesus, she felt a renewed sense of purpose and clarity. Navigating the dating world as a Christian wasn't without its challenges, but with her values, boundaries, and trust in God, she was better equipped to seek the love story He had planned for her. She knew that the journey ahead might be filled with ups and downs, but she was prepared to face it with faith, hope, and the support of her Christian community.

4

Building a Christ-Centered Relationship

Title: "Love Letters to Jesus: Christian Dating Devotions"

Emily's journey had taken her through self-reflection, the cultivation of patience, and the navigation of the dating world. Now, in Chapter 4, she was ready to explore the core of her quest: building a Christ-centered relationship.

1. The Foundation of Prayer and Communication

As Emily entered a new relationship, she understood the importance of maintaining a strong foundation of prayer and open communication. In her love letter to Jesus, she wrote:

"Dear Jesus,

I am grateful for the person You have brought into my life, someone who shares my faith and values. Help us, Lord, to make our relationship centered on You from the very beginning.

Guide us to communicate openly and honestly, to discuss our dreams, fears, and plans, and to share our spiritual journeys with one another. May our words be seasoned with love and understanding, just as You intended.

We also commit our relationship to prayer, seeking Your guidance and wisdom every step of the way. We know that by placing You at the center of our relationship, we can build a strong and lasting love.

Amen."

2. Fostering Spiritual Growth Together

Emily understood that a Christ-centered relationship should be a catalyst for both partners' spiritual growth. She expressed this in her love letter:

"Dear Jesus,

I recognize that the purpose of a Christ-centered relationship isn't just about companionship but also about helping each other grow closer to You. We want to be a source of support and encouragement in our respective journeys of faith.

Guide us, Lord, to engage in spiritual activities together, such as attending church, studying the Bible, and praying. Help us to hold each other accountable and challenge one another to become better Christians.

May our love be a testament to Your grace, and may our relationship inspire others to seek a faith-filled love like ours.

Amen."

3. Practicing Grace and Forgiveness

Emily knew that even in a Christ-centered relationship, there would be moments of conflict and misunderstanding. She asked for guidance in handling these situations:

"Dear Jesus,

In our relationship, we commit to practicing grace and forgiveness, just as You have shown us. We understand that we are imperfect, and there will be moments of tension and disagreement. But help us to approach these moments with love and patience.

Teach us to forgive one another as You have forgiven us. Grant us the wisdom to address issues with humility and understanding, seeking reconciliation and growth.

We want our love to be a reflection of Your love, which is boundless and forgiving.

Amen."

4. Trusting in God's Plan for the Future

As Emily's relationship continued to grow, she held onto her faith and trust in God's plan:

"Dear Jesus,

We know that You have a purpose for our relationship, and we trust in Your plan for our future. Whether it leads to marriage or another path, we know that it is part of Your divine design.

Help us to be patient and content in the season we find ourselves in, and may Your will be done in our lives. We place our relationship in Your hands, knowing that with You at the center, our love story will be beautiful and meaningful.

Amen."

With this love letter, Emily and her partner embarked on their journey of building a Christ-centered relationship. Their commitment to prayer, open communication, spiritual growth, grace, and trust in God's plan would be the guiding lights as they continued to explore their love story rooted in faith.

5

Nurturing a Love that Reflects God's Love

Title: "Love Letters to Jesus: Christian Dating Devotions"

Emily had journeyed through self-reflection, patience, the dating world, and the development of a Christ-centered relationship. Now, in Chapter 5, her focus shifted to nurturing and maintaining a love that reflected the love of God.

1. The Importance of Gratitude

In her love letter to Jesus, Emily expressed her gratitude for the love she had found:

"Dear Jesus,

I'm overwhelmed with gratitude for the love You've brought into my life. This relationship is a blessing, and I'm constantly reminded of Your goodness and love through it.

Help me to express my gratitude not only to my partner but also to You.

Remind me that every good and perfect gift comes from above, and may I always be thankful for the love You've given me.

Amen."

2. The Power of Intentionality

Emily recognized the need for intentionality in nurturing her relationship. She wrote:

"Dear Jesus,

I want to be intentional in my love, just as You were intentional in Your love for us. Help me to put effort into our relationship, to plan meaningful dates, to listen with an open heart, and to prioritize my partner.

Guide me in showing love through small gestures, words of affirmation, and acts of kindness. I know that love is not just a feeling but an action, and I want to act in a way that honors You.

Amen."

3. Weathering Life's Storms Together

Emily acknowledged that life could be challenging, and she sought the strength to face these challenges with her partner:

"Dear Jesus,

Life is filled with ups and downs, and I know that our relationship will face its share of storms. But with You at our side, we can weather any tempest.

Help us to face challenges with faith, love, and resilience. May our love be a shelter in the storm, a refuge of comfort, and a source of strength.

Teach us to support and love one another during difficult times, just as You have supported and loved us.

Amen."

4. Maintaining Individuality and Independence

Emily knew the importance of maintaining her own identity while being part of a couple:

"Dear Jesus,

I recognize the importance of maintaining my individuality within this relationship. Help me to continue growing as an individual and pursuing my passions, just as I support my partner in their pursuits.

Guide us in finding a balance between togetherness and independence. May our love enhance our lives without suffocating our individuality.

Amen."

5. A Love that Radiates God's Love

Emily's ultimate desire was to have a love that radiated God's love to the world:

"Dear Jesus,

Above all, I pray that our love will be a beacon of Your love to others. May the way we love, support, and respect each other draw others closer to You.

Guide us to be a testimony of Your grace, compassion, and forgiveness in the way we treat one another. May our love inspire others to seek the love that can only be found in You.

Amen."

With these intentions in mind, Emily continued her journey, nurturing a love that reflected the love of God. She knew that, with Jesus as the center of their relationship, she and her partner could continue to grow and thrive in a love that was truly extraordinary.

6

Facing Challenges and Growing Together

Title: "Love Letters to Jesus: Christian Dating Devotions"

As Emily's love story continued to unfold, she realized that the journey of a Christ-centered relationship wasn't without its challenges. Chapter 6 in her dating devotions would focus on facing these difficulties and growing together through them.

1. Communication in Conflict

In her love letter to Jesus, Emily acknowledged the importance of effective communication during times of conflict:

"Dear Jesus,

Conflict is a natural part of any relationship, but I want to handle it in a way that honors You. Help us communicate openly, honestly, and respectfully when we face disagreements.

Guide us to listen to each other with love and understanding, to express our feelings and needs without judgment, and to seek reconciliation. May our conflicts be opportunities for growth and deepening our connection.

Amen."

2. Forgiveness and Grace

Emily recognized the need for forgiveness and grace in their relationship:

"Dear Jesus,

I understand that forgiveness and grace are essential in any relationship. Teach us to forgive one another as You have forgiven us. Help us to extend grace and compassion when we make mistakes or hurt each other.

May our relationship be characterized by humility, repentance, and a willingness to heal and grow. We want our love to mirror Your love, which is rich in mercy and forgiveness.

Amen."

3. Overcoming External Pressures

Emily and her partner were not immune to external pressures and influences. She asked for strength to protect their relationship:

"Dear Jesus,

In the face of external pressures and influences, help us to stand strong in our faith and commitment to each other. Guide us to protect our relationship from negative influences that could harm the love we share.

May our love be a sanctuary, a place of safety and growth, and may we always prioritize our faith and relationship above all else.

Amen."

4. Encouraging Individual Growth

While nurturing their love, Emily wanted to ensure they both continued to grow as individuals:

"Dear Jesus,

I pray that we continue to grow as individuals within our relationship. Help us pursue our passions, dreams, and personal growth, even as we support and encourage one another.

Guide us in finding a balance between togetherness and individuality. May our love enhance our lives and empower us to become the best versions of ourselves.

Amen."

5. Trusting in God's Plan

Throughout their challenges, Emily maintained her trust in God's plan:

"Dear Jesus,

In the midst of challenges, we trust in Your plan for our relationship. You brought us together for a reason, and we believe that Your hand is guiding our love story.

Help us to face challenges with faith and hope, knowing that Your will is unfolding in our lives. We place our relationship in Your capable hands and seek Your wisdom in all we do.

Amen."

With these intentions and prayers, Emily and her partner were ready to face challenges head-on, knowing that their love story was a journey of faith, growth, and love. They had learned that, with Jesus at the center, they could overcome anything and continue to nurture a love that reflected His divine love.

7

Celebrating Milestones and Looking Ahead

Title: "Love Letters to Jesus: Christian Dating Devotions"

Emily and her partner had come a long way in their Christ-centered relationship. In Chapter 7 of their dating devotions, they celebrated their milestones and looked ahead to the future.

1. Reflecting on the Journey

In her love letter to Jesus, Emily took a moment to reflect on the journey they had been on:

"Dear Jesus,

As we celebrate the milestones of our relationship, I can't help but look back and see the incredible journey You've led us on. From self-reflection to the challenges we've faced and overcome, our love story is a testament to Your grace and guidance.

Thank You for being the cornerstone of our relationship, for helping us navigate challenges, and for teaching us the true meaning of love. We are so grateful for Your presence in our lives.

Amen."

2. Gratitude for Each Other

Emily expressed her gratitude for the love they shared:

"Dear Jesus,

I am immensely grateful for the person You've brought into my life. They are a gift from You, and I cherish the love we share.

Help us to always appreciate and express our gratitude for one another. May our words and actions be a constant reminder of the love You've blessed us with.

Amen."

3. Setting Goals for the Future

Emily and her partner knew that their journey wasn't over; they had more to explore and discover together:

"Dear Jesus,

As we celebrate our love, we also look forward to the future. Guide us in setting goals, both individually and as a couple. We want our relationship to be a source of inspiration and growth for each other.

Help us to dream together, make plans, and pursue our shared goals. May our love be a driving force in accomplishing Your purpose for our lives.

Amen."

4. Strengthening Commitment

Emily reaffirmed her commitment to her partner and to God:

"Dear Jesus,

I want to reiterate my commitment to both You and my partner. Our love is a reflection of Your divine love, and I am dedicated to nurturing and growing it.

Guide us to strengthen our commitment to each other, to be loyal and faithful, and to honor the vows we've made in our hearts. May our love be unshakeable in the face of life's challenges.

Amen."

5. Trusting in God's Plan for the Future

Throughout their reflections and celebrations, Emily and her partner held onto their trust in God's plan:

"Dear Jesus,

We trust in Your plan for our future. As we look ahead, we know that Your hand is guiding our love story. Whether it leads to marriage, a lifelong partnership, or another path, we have faith that it is part of Your divine design.

Help us to remain patient, content, and open to the adventures You have in store. We place our relationship and our future in Your capable hands.

Amen."

With these intentions and prayers, Emily and her partner celebrated their milestones, thanked God for the love they shared, and looked ahead with hope and trust. They knew that their journey, with Jesus at the center, was a beautiful testament to the power of faith, love, and devotion.

8

A Lifetime of Love

Title: "Love Letters to Jesus: Christian Dating Devotions"

Emily and her partner had reached a significant point in their journey—a commitment to a lifetime of love. In Chapter 8 of their dating devotions, they reflected on the journey they had taken, the love they shared, and the commitment they were making to each other.

1. A Journey of Faith

In her love letter to Jesus, Emily acknowledged the importance of faith in their journey:

"Dear Jesus,

As we stand at this crossroads of commitment, we look back on our journey with hearts filled with gratitude. You have been our guiding light, our source of strength, and the foundation of our love.

Through every trial, challenge, and joy, our faith has grown, and we have drawn closer to You. We understand that our love story is not just about us but about glorifying You.

Amen."

2. The Covenant of Marriage

Emily and her partner were preparing for the sacrament of marriage, a commitment before God and their loved ones:

"Dear Jesus,

As we prepare to enter the sacred covenant of marriage, we understand the weight and significance of this commitment. Marriage is not just a legal contract but a spiritual union, a reflection of Your love for the Church.

Guide us in the preparation for this holy sacrament, helping us to approach it with humility and reverence. May our marriage be a shining example of Your love, grace, and fidelity.

Amen."

3. Embracing the Challenges

They knew that their journey would continue to be filled with challenges, but they were committed to facing them together:

"Dear Jesus,

We understand that marriage is not without its challenges. But we are committed to facing them together, with faith, love, and unwavering support for one another.

Help us to remember that our love is strong, not because it has never been tested, but because it has survived and thrived through trials. We are prepared to meet any obstacle with the strength that comes from You.

Amen."

4. Building a Christ-Centered Home

Emily and her partner wanted to build a home that reflected their love for Jesus:

"Dear Jesus,

As we start this new chapter, we desire to build a home that is centered on You. May our love for each other be a testament to Your grace and mercy, and may our home be a place of peace, love, and spiritual growth.

Guide us to create a Christ-centered family, one that nurtures faith, love, and understanding. May our home be a sanctuary where we can grow closer to You and each other.

Amen."

5. A Lifetime of Love

As they stood on the threshold of a lifelong commitment, Emily and her partner reaffirmed their love for each other and for Jesus:

"Dear Jesus,

We commit to a lifetime of love, rooted in You. May our marriage be a reflection of Your divine love, rich in compassion, forgiveness, and unwavering commitment.

Help us to continue growing in love for each other and for You. May our journey together be a testament to the power of faith, love, and devotion.

Amen."

With these intentions and prayers, Emily and her partner embarked on the lifelong journey of marriage, ready to face whatever challenges and joys lay ahead with faith, love, and the knowledge that Jesus would always be at the center of their love story.

9

The Power of Prayer and Perseverance

Title: "Love Letters to Jesus: Christian Dating Devotions"

Emily and her partner were now married and had embarked on their lifelong journey together. In Chapter 9 of their dating devotions, they focused on the importance of prayer, perseverance, and their unwavering commitment to one another and to Jesus.

1. A Strong Foundation of Prayer

In her love letter to Jesus, Emily reflected on the significance of prayer in their marriage:

"Dear Jesus,

Prayer has been the cornerstone of our love story, and it remains the cornerstone of our marriage. We thank You for the gift of communication with You and for the power of prayer.

Guide us to continue to seek Your guidance and wisdom in our daily lives, especially in the choices we make as a married couple. May our prayers be a source of strength and unity, a way for us to seek Your will in all we do.

Amen."

2. Perseverance Through Challenges

They knew that challenges would continue to arise, and they were committed to persevering through them:

"Dear Jesus,

In the face of challenges, we are reminded of the importance of perseverance. We are committed to standing strong together, even when life tests our love and faith.

Help us to remember that challenges are opportunities for growth and strength. Guide us in facing them with faith, grace, and unwavering support for each other.

Amen."

3. A Love that Overcomes

Emily and her partner were determined to let their love overcome any obstacle:

"Dear Jesus,

Our love is a testimony to Your grace, and we are determined to let it overcome any obstacle that may come our way. May our love be a source of strength, forgiveness, and resilience.

Guide us in embracing our commitment to love unconditionally, just as You have loved us. May our love shine as a beacon of hope and inspiration for others.

Amen."

4. Growing Together in Faith

They were committed to growing together in faith as they grew together in marriage:

"Dear Jesus,

As we journey through this marriage, we also seek to grow together in faith. Help us to support each other's spiritual journeys and to encourage one another to draw closer to You.

Guide us in our shared devotion, in studying Your Word, and in nurturing our individual relationships with You. May our faith continue to be the foundation of our love.

Amen."

5. Looking Ahead with Hope

With their unwavering commitment to each other and to Jesus, they looked ahead to the future with hope:

"Dear Jesus,

As we look ahead, we do so with hope and faith in Your plan. We trust that our journey, with You at the center, will continue to be a beautiful love story.

Guide us in our dreams and aspirations, and may our marriage be a source of joy and inspiration to others. May our love be a reflection of Your love, which is eternal and full of grace.

Amen."

In this chapter, Emily and her partner affirmed their dedication to prayer, perseverance, and their commitment to Jesus, ensuring that their marriage would remain strong and their love would continue to flourish. They knew that their love story was a testimony to the power of faith, love, and devotion.

10

A Legacy of Love

Title: "Love Letters to Jesus: Christian Dating Devotions"

Emily and her partner had journeyed through various phases of their relationship, from dating to marriage and beyond. In Chapter 10 of their dating devotions, they focused on the legacy of love they hoped to leave behind for generations to come.

1. Reflecting on a Life Together

In her love letter to Jesus, Emily took a moment to reflect on the life they had built together:

"Dear Jesus,

As we look back on the years we've spent together, we are filled with gratitude for the life we've built, the love we've shared, and the family we've created.

Thank You for being the anchor of our love story, for guiding us through the storms and helping us celebrate the joys. We are profoundly grateful for the life we've lived together.

Amen."

2. Passing Down Faith and Values

Emily and her partner recognized the importance of passing down their faith and values to their children and future generations:

"Dear Jesus,

We desire to leave a legacy of faith and love for our children and their children. Help us to instill in them the values and beliefs that have been the foundation of our love.

Guide us in teaching them about Your love and grace, and may our family be a testament to the power of a Christ-centered home. May our children continue to walk in the light of faith and love, just as we have.

Amen."

3. A Source of Wisdom and Guidance

They knew that their love story would serve as a source of wisdom and guidance for their loved ones:

"Dear Jesus,

May our love story be a source of wisdom and guidance for our family and friends. Help us to share our experiences, challenges, and triumphs with those who look to us for advice and inspiration.

Guide us in being a source of encouragement and support for others in their own relationships. May our love continue to be a beacon of hope for those who seek a love grounded in faith.

Amen."

4. A Beacon of Hope for Others

Emily and her partner aspired to inspire others to pursue Christ-centered love:

"Dear Jesus,

We hope that our love story will inspire others to seek the beauty and depth of a Christ-centered relationship. May our journey be a beacon of hope for those who are searching for love rooted in faith.

Guide us in being ambassadors of Your love, showing others the power of a love that is rich in compassion, forgiveness, and grace. May our love inspire others to seek a love story that is centered on You.

Amen."

5. Looking Back with Thankfulness

With hearts full of gratitude, they looked back on their journey:

"Dear Jesus,

As we look back on our love story, we do so with hearts full of gratitude. Thank You for leading us on this path, for guiding us through every phase of our relationship, and for being the constant source of strength and love in our lives.

Amen."

In this final chapter, Emily and her partner reflected on the legacy of love they hoped to leave behind for their family, friends, and anyone seeking a love that is deeply rooted in faith and devotion to Jesus. Their love story was a testament to the power of faith, love, and commitment.

11

Endless Love and Gratitude

Title: "Love Letters to Jesus: Christian Dating Devotions"

Emily and her partner had journeyed through a life filled with faith, love, and devotion to Jesus. In Chapter 11 of their dating devotions, they focused on their endless love and gratitude for the journey they had taken and the love they had shared.

1. A Love That Knows No Bounds

In her love letter to Jesus, Emily marveled at the boundless love that had sustained them:

"Dear Jesus,

Our love knows no bounds, and it is a testament to Your grace and guidance. We've faced challenges, celebrated milestones, and journeyed together through life, all with You at the center.

Our love is a reflection of Your love, which is endless and unwavering. Thank You for being the cornerstone of our love story.

Amen."

2. Gratitude for Every Moment

Emily expressed her gratitude for every moment they had shared together:

"Dear Jesus,

In every moment, we are grateful for the life we've created together. From the small everyday joys to the major milestones, our journey has been rich and meaningful.

Thank You for blessing us with each day, for guiding us in our choices, and for helping us grow in love and faith. We are eternally thankful for the life we've lived together.

Amen."

3. Love as a Source of Strength

They recognized the role love played as a source of strength:

"Dear Jesus,

Our love has been a wellspring of strength, helping us to face life's challenges with grace and faith. We've supported each other through trials, celebrated one another's successes, and faced each day with a sense of unity and purpose.

Help us to continue to rely on our love as a source of courage, comfort, and support. May our love remain a beacon of hope, not just for us but for all who witness it.

Amen."

4. Faithful Commitment

Emily and her partner reaffirmed their commitment to each other and to their faith:

"Dear Jesus,

We reaffirm our commitment to one another and to You. Our love is steadfast, grounded in faith, and unyielding in its devotion.

Guide us to continue to prioritize our relationship and our faith, to stand strong together and to support one another in our journeys. Our commitment to You and to each other is unwavering.

Amen."

5. Looking Ahead with Hope

With endless love and gratitude, they looked ahead to the future:

"Dear Jesus,

As we look to the future, we do so with hope, faith, and endless love. We trust in Your plan, and we know that our journey, with You at the center, will continue to be a beautiful love story.

Guide us in our dreams, aspirations, and the legacy we hope to leave behind. May our love shine as a beacon of Your grace and love for generations to come.

Amen."

In this final chapter, Emily and her partner celebrated their endless love and gratitude for the journey they had taken, recognizing that their love story was a testament to the power of faith, love, and devotion to Jesus. Their commitment was unwavering, and their hope for the future was boundless.

12

A Journey of Worship and Ongoing Devotion

Title: "Love Letters to Jesus: Christian Dating Devotions"

As Emily and her partner continued to walk hand in hand on their lifelong journey of faith and love, they recognized the importance of worship and ongoing devotion to Jesus in Chapter 12 of their dating devotions.

1. Gratitude for the Journey

In her love letter to Jesus, Emily began with a heartfelt expression of gratitude:

"Dear Jesus,

Our journey together has been a remarkable one, filled with Your grace, guidance, and unwavering love. As we reflect on the path we've walked, we can't help but be filled with gratitude for Your presence.

Thank You for being the center of our love story, for leading us through the trials, and for illuminating the joys in our lives. Our love is a testament to Your faithfulness.

Amen."

2. Worship as a Bond of Unity

Emily and her partner saw worship as a bond that strengthened their unity:

"Dear Jesus,

Worship has been a bond that has drawn us closer together. As we come before You in reverence and awe, we find our hearts aligned and our spirits connected in love for You.

Guide us in our worship, both individually and as a couple. May our shared faith and devotion to You continue to be the foundation of our relationship.

Amen."

3. Growing Together in Faith

They were committed to growing together in faith and understanding:

"Dear Jesus,

As we continue our journey together, we want to grow together in our faith and understanding of Your Word. Help us to nurture our spiritual lives individually and as a couple.

Guide us to study Your Word, pray together, and support one another in our spiritual journeys. May our love be a reflection of Your love, which is grounded in faith, wisdom, and grace.

Amen."

4. The Power of Prayer

Prayer was an integral part of their love story, and it remained at the forefront of their relationship:

"Dear Jesus,

Our love story has been marked by the power of prayer, and we know that it will continue to be a source of strength and guidance for us.

Help us to remain faithful in our prayers, both for each other and for our shared journey. May our prayers be a bridge that connects us to You and to each other, and may they be a constant source of wisdom and grace.

Amen."

5. Looking Ahead with Hope

With hearts full of hope, they looked ahead to the future:

"Dear Jesus,

As we look to the future, we do so with hope, faith, and ongoing devotion to You. We know that our journey, with You at the center, will continue to be a testament to the power of faith, love, and devotion.

Guide us in our dreams, aspirations, and the legacy we hope to leave behind. May our love be an everlasting source of Your grace and love for generations to come.

Amen."

In this final chapter, Emily and her partner celebrated their ongoing journey of worship and devotion to Jesus. They recognized that their love story was a testament to the power of faith, love, and unwavering commitment. Their hope for the future was boundless, and their devotion was eternal.

Title: Love Letters to Jesus: Christian Dating Devotions

Book Summary:

"Love Letters to Jesus: Christian Dating Devotions" is a heartfelt and inspiring journey of love, faith, and devotion centered around the Christian dating experience. The book follows the life and love story of Emily, a young Christian woman seeking a relationship that reflects her unwavering faith and commitment to Jesus.

The book is divided into twelve chapters, each focusing on different aspects of the Christian dating journey, from self-reflection to marriage and beyond. Emily's story is woven together with the love letters she writes to Jesus, expressing her hopes, fears, and desires as she navigates the complexities of dating as a Christian.

Throughout the chapters, readers witness Emily's personal growth, as well as her evolving relationship with her partner. They explore essential themes such as defining values and boundaries, seeking compatibility and shared faith, practicing patience and trust in God's plan, and nurturing a love that reflects God's love.

Emily's journey continues into marriage, family, and the legacy of love she and her partner hope to leave behind. The book emphasizes the importance of prayer, perseverance, and ongoing devotion to Jesus as the foundation of a strong and enduring Christian relationship.

"Love Letters to Jesus" offers valuable insights, advice, and spiritual guidance for Christians seeking to build meaningful, Christ-centered relationships. Through Emily's heartfelt love letters and experiences, readers are reminded of the power of faith, love, and devotion to Jesus in creating lasting and fulfilling love stories.

This book serves as a source of inspiration for individuals looking to navigate the challenges and joys of Christian dating while keeping their faith and love for Jesus at the heart of their journey.

www.ingramcontent.com/pod-product-compliance
Lightning Source LLC
LaVergne TN
LVHW010437070526
838199LV00066B/6057